I0441084

Hypnosis and Mind Control

Christophe Pank

Author of :

1/ My first steps on the Law of Attraction (Feb 2013)

2/ Journey of a Hypnosis practitioner against cancer (Fev 2015)

3/ Hypnosis and Pain Management : The study of the Hypno-Analgesia Process (Jul 2015)

4/ Limited Power : Accepting our own limits is to open up our real potential (May 2016)

5/Hypnosis and Hypnotic Gastric Band (Jan 2017)

6/ Hyperempiria and Self-Mastery : Apply Hyperempiria for your personal development (Jul 2017)

7/ Energetics CT (Sept 2017)

8/ Easy Self Hypnosis Techniques (Jan 2018)

9/ Power of Loser (April 2018)

10/ Learn To decide (May 2018)

Introduction

I personally like the manipulation and influence subject. I'd like to admit from the beginning, **I am a manipulator and I act like a jerk every day of my life,** in a more or less conscious way. At first, it does not give a particularly positive image in a society where we criticize men of influence, the lies of international companies, and the various frauds. *We like to sell the image of a society 'good, egalitarian and moral'.* However, when we speak to many people, there is often the desire for control that resurfaces. To control a situation, to control the risks that the children can take, to control the emotions or the reactions of this or this person. In short, we have **a natural propensity to want to manipulate, even to control the world** around us and even more the people with whom we live. To persuade you, observe the children in the playgrounds, some dominate by their physics, others by their intelligence, others by their beauty, others by their kindness or by their malice. Often they come together in different groups that do not have the same levers of manipulation and influence. We can find exceptions, only this essay is about *a generalized reality . If this perception did not exist, there would not be as many writers who would write books on defense against manipulators and manipulations on all sides.* Most are **best sellers** therefore, many feel this 'reality'. For my part, my goal is to offer you to assume that you are manipulators and not only when it is for the 'good'.

Assume that we are assholes and that we do many actions for us and only us. Positive justifications are put in place after, when the possible idea of guilt hatches in our mind.

Experience has shown me that to say that we are ALL manipulators put a lot of cold in conferences and meetings. Often, the most virulent people to defend themselves, to want to show that the intention simply just and positive, unconditionally ... **are the most manipulative.** For some, this test will make you bristle. You will surely tell you that Pank is really a big idiot who thinks he's for whom ... and you'll be right. First idea to keep in mind, if you accept to be a conscious or unconscious manipulator, you must accept that many people will hate you or at least not love you. The interesting question after that is ... could I manipulate them to love me, or at least to appreciate myself enough to ... **train them where I want** ? This test is therefore field oriented, *I will not detail complex techniques* , **just simple and effective** , to allow you to become aware of many strategies that you put in place and especially to assume to apply them.These methods represent **covered hypnosis** it is a practice resulting from NLP and conversational hypnosis, which aims to influence and guide the most subtle possible interlocutors. No secrets, only it will be necessary to put into practice and to ask you the good questions. Are you ready to assume?

1/ Conscious Manipulation vs. Unconscious Manipulation

The paradigm of this book is to say that **we are all manipulators in our daily lives** . If this idea is tingling you a little, it is surely that you manipulate your thought enough for yourself, so as not to be aware of your own vices. And **you are worse than the famous perverse narcissists,** so much put forward in our world complementary disciplines like brief therapies. A person who accepts what she does, is not necessarily better, but she has at least the sincerity to know what she practices and not to sell *a false image of herself to others* ... on this point, she does not manipulate or rather *she handles less* . So we like to tell ourselves that we are not manipulating, rather than influencing. As you know, I am in the world of hypnosis and complementary disciplines. **Hypnosis is the art of manipulation draped in the guise of benevolent influence for the well-being of the partners.** I have come to hypnosis via Neuro Linguistic Programming, which is actually a conversational hypnosis. Its founders had the lucidity to pass their method as a system to communicate better ... while it is a method to better train the interlocutors where we wish, without they can judge that we are the ones who guide them . I wanted to understand humans and how they work. Certainly out of fear, misunderstanding and wanting to interact better with them. I am a very combative personality, which makes me see the world as a war. So understand that NLP tools, then hypnosis, **offered me a lot of ammunition in my relationship with my peers** .

When today I ask hypnotists and hypnosis practitioners why they started this discipline, the vast majority will express the idea that it is to help with an effective tool. *We are lucky, rented is the sky, thousands of people each year are formed in hypnosis for the sake of their neighbor, I will add Hallelujah !!!* Help with hypnosis ... we can help in many ways, we can even choose many other disciplines to support others. Of course, **it's an innocuous choice, hypnosis.** To practice it for a long time and having made thousands of pretalk (presentation of what is hypnosis in order to live a more or less short term experience) whether in the evening, on the street, in the office and wherever possible, the vast majority (a study * shows that 83% of people who hear about hypnosis, think about mind control and manipulation) see *hypnosis as a way to get into each other's head* . Luckily, in schools and for people interested in hypnosis, the motivation to start is to help others with an effective tool ... There is a beautiful self-manipulation is not it? It's hard to say that what interests us *is to be able to do as Messmer and "to sleep" the other to reprogram.* **It's less glamorous** . Although it is not necessarily this idea, the motivation is, almost all the time, related to this notion of influence that we can have on people who are not well. Many practitioners are deeply angry when they can not save and change their partners in the office. Even if in school, we keep saying that it's *the partner who will go where he can* , **this feeling of helplessness** is a recurring element. Simply because we think we're going to tamper with their beliefs and others, and then that **everything will be better thanks to us.** The customer is better, that's what matters, right? Yes, only that makes many of us **unconscious manipulators**.

Let's get out of the frame of the help to the person, when we see a friend who is not doing well and that we seek by 'empathy' to calm him, soothe him, *who would like to support us?* If we had not been in contact with him we would not have been in an empathic movement, so free. By cons, in direct contact, we live things in us: 'I do not like to see you like that', 'I understand what you live', etc ... are sentences that we exploit many times. If the other stops or reduces his suffering, what happens with ours? **We want others to do better so that we feel better.** So we have developed a lot of strategies, more or less effective that allow for reduced stress and especially a calming of the common trance. **We handle.** Yes for a good cause, yes for compassion, yes, yes and re-yes ...

All that remains is an excuse not to admit that we have been pointing to what WE looked good.

That's what I call unconscious manipulation and if we bring it out into the open, we have a *argument that we did it with a good intention, that we want the other to go well* ... Why not accept that millions of people are not well at the same time and that **we have nothing to beat** ? It's different because we know it? If we had no emotional receptivity we would act the same way?

Young children understand very quickly that kisses and a smile are stimuli strong enough for an adult to take care of them, if not a little crying and emergencies happen (in the case no pain). *In our entry into this world we have put in place strategies to first survive* .

Manipulate and influence are survival tools it is very reptilian as operation, it is for this reason that *we are all easily tempted by this dark side* (which I find particularly brilliant). There is no more dependent than a baby or a young child (often to the pleasure of many parents). **Handle emotions** is one of the most useful techniques to have a quick return of attention, the most interesting is that no matter the positive or negative emotion, the important will be the attention. Even a bullying is a way to perceive a positive return on the method adopted. For some babies some will talk to me instinctively to justify the manipulation of future experts.

So let's take a child who wants to ask one thing from his parents, he uses most of the time **kindness and reciprocity** . Two levers that I'm sure you've used thousands of times. By giving a kiss or an act of tenderness, we created a breach in the other and in our cultures, *an unconscious duty to return all or part of this gift* . Added to this is a voice and semantics that lead to *kindness. This lowers defenses and mistrust* of the vast majority of humans, if it is not excessive or disproportionate to the lived situation. There is for children this notion of: he is cute, he is kind, he makes efforts ... retranscribable in the adult, he takes the tweezers, he is benevolent, he is good. **All these phrases and ideas are bullshit to self-validate the reasons for our acceptance or, better still, our inability to say no at that time.** As I said before, we are always justified when we are manipulated to give a conscious, coherent and analytical reason.

This is the principle of hypnosis which many participants, especially in hypnosis street and stage, explain that they could not do what is asked ... yes it's true but they did. The idea of manipulation is not to forget or pass an idea without the other noticing, but simply that the other goes where we had decided, it can be a thousand and One way, putting a gun on someone's temple is physical manipulation, promising a gift if we do something is an emotional manipulation.

The possibilities are unlimited and depending on the facilities we have in this or that area, we exploit some forms more than others. How many times have you been nice to get something? How many times have you returned *a service to receive another later, with the famous: 'But me I was there for you'* ....

So are you still people who never handle? Or are you completely unaware of this process, or even assumed?

* Alternative technique, classic soft science like hypnosis, the word 'study' gives the idea of seriousness and makes it easier to accept the idea that is proposed. In this case, I do not know any study on this subject.

2/ Dare to be an asshole !!
Induce trances.

"Ah no, mad me peace, Pank, I am a good person and even if I have my vices, I do not want to manipulate others !! For what? Because Daddy was manipulating? Or Mom? Who gave you such a negative image of the manipulation? As a reminder, physical or verbal violence is a strategy of manipulation. Maybe it's spiritual virtue ... *Let's talk about these spiritualities that continue to manipulate our minds in temples, churches, mosques or synagogues.* We go through a means that we discussed at the end of the chapter. **The substitution...**We pass the messages we want under the guise of a book and an interpreter to speak on behalf of the great Boss. With this manipulation we manage to create wars, violence, hatred or intolerance. Be careful, I do not say that spirituality brings only negative. This substitution, that is to say take a reference figure (and here in this case the BOSS, the most up-to-the-point entity, which we refer to as giving directions) can help to develop self-help, forgiveness, love **in the FAITH** . **Faith is the most powerful lever of manipulative trance** . I will come back to it shortly. Before that, I'll give you ideas that work well to use substitution, you've already exploited it many times.

For example, mothers who threaten to tell the father when he comes home, *she substitutes her faltering authority* of the moment by an outside entity whose **can 'fantasize' the consequences** .

The strength of this technique is to help not get wet because **it's not us but another** who has said or expressed an idea, and in addition it allows to put his interlocutor in **a projective model** , so that depending on the tone we give to our substitution, we turn to negative ideas or positive idealizations. **The less precise we are, the more we let the other put what he wants according to his emotional state of the moment.** So enjoy being **not specific** as PNL likes to call it, to imagine the consequences of the threat. I like the **'You'll see ... one day'.** This one is doubly dirty, because we do not know the consequences of the repercussions and, in terms of the timeline, we are unable to know if it is for soon or if we must be on our guard over the months or the years to come. Another example, **to pass an idea through a book,** an author or a scientific study ... This one is so common. 'I read in ... I saw a report that ... An article explained precisely ... Mr E. explained that the technique was like that ... *Your answer in your head should be: Shut up, I'm asking you what you think, not your reference* . Often it intervenes in conversations to support an argument, as if our interlocutor with his own ideas and comments had to support with a referent.

You begin to understand what I'm saying because like **confirms understanding specialist Tommy Duwan** after several examples everything fits easily and quickly. The objective of this technique is therefore to allow a decrease in judgment. In **Elmanian hypnosis** and direct, we pay specific attention to what we call **the critical factor** . To put it simply, our conscious is able to analyze and make logical just about everything we live.

It is for this reason that *we have the ability to justify, even when we are manipulative or manipulated, the positive intent of things* . Our subconscious is our hard drive that safeguards long-term memories, emotions, automatic patterns of our lives, values and beliefs. Between the two, most of the time, you have **the critical factor** that we can also name the **judgmental capacity** . This is why when you have a decision to make, you make a decision that seems right after a quick dialogue between past experiences and the coherent information of the moment (dialogue between the conscious and the subconscious, led by the jugement). Influence and manipulation induce **a decrease in the capacity of judgment,** I say once more: **decrease** . It is rare, even if it can happen sometimes, that this critical factor disappears completely. This decrease in the critical factor is what we call **an induction** in hypnosis, which leads *towards a communication without the barrier of judgment, which one names **trance** .*

To be clear, in a trance we have the ability to analyze things, only **we are less and less inclined to objectively judge the different options presented** . The goal of our manipulative acts is therefore *to put in trance* our interlocutors to guide them with information that becomes suggestions. Faith, which I mentioned earlier, is **the most powerful inductive principle** . In a few moments if you speak of God, Jesus, Mohamed, Buddha or Yahweh to people cradled in these cultures, there will be a lessening of their judgment, the object of substitution, the book for example or a prophecy, the causing in *a trance connected to their long-term memories and automated models, such as a sign of the cross or bless the Prophet Mohamed.*

We can very well analyze our gestures and rituals, yet we have not judged them for a long time, **there is an absolute validation** . Faith can of course be oriented to many other things than religion. We can have faith in friends, family, money and millions of other elements. **Faith is an absolute,** there are no questions, people just tell us they know. **Moreover the questioning of this idea is completely impossible ... without a long work of manipulation to create ... the DOUBT** . Moreover, in religions, it is said to never doubt ... from a manipulation point of view, it is a superb suggestion to stay in the process started and have an automated response to external stimuli given by referents.

If you do not want to adhere to manipulation and become an asshole, I invite you to stop reading now ... and you will have paid this book for a few pages, otherwise you can continue and therefore by conscious choice **adhere to the immoral contract of becoming an assumed manipulator.** In one way or another do you feel free in your choices of what will follow now? To become this conscious manipulator, it is essential to know **put in trance** . And rest assured, you who are **passive manipulators** you have done it thousands of times without the slightest awareness of the tool used. Here are the three ways to create a trance:

- **Internal focus :** that is to say, orient our interlocutors towards a path that brings them back to them. The idea is to search them in the subconscious, memories, emotions, patterns, values or beliefs.

The more we do this internal scan the more we reduce the ability to judge information coming from outside, so we open a gap.

- **Confusion and saturation:** that is to say train the mind to no longer be able to take all the information. This can be done with two different techniques that we have used to bring together. **The confusion** which offers links and information that we are not able to fully understand, especially with non-specific languages that lead to search internally (internal focus) explanations and meanings.

  Saturation which gives so much information that our processing capacity can no longer respond and it is as if we are going into denial of service.

- **Pattern break** : that is to say, the interruption of an automatic model, which your interlocutor is not necessarily aware of. This opens a gap and a questioning of the judgment that is lost in this bug a few moments.

You have used these strategies many times to get what you want. For example, when you are on **emotional manipulation** with your spouse on a reminder of the good times you spent on vacation, when you were both without children, to imply that it would be nice to have a good time both. This is a classic use of **focusing,** with all the details of the sea, the beach, the morning sleep etc. When you **are drinking your buddies** on a place where you want to eat and they abandon the trade so you have saturated them, even if they are not necessarily motivated.

Or when children are trying to negotiate and you are doing **an immediate transition to the newsletter** you have just received, interrupting the proposed arguments. In our daily lives, we use inductions and the trances of our colleagues, our friends or our family, to guide where it is most comfortable for us.

Being part of the circle of manipulators assumed, I am sure you would like to know which lever you can use to exploit **this flaw** .

3/ Make an information, a suggestion oriented

A good manipulator assumed like you, must recognize that there are strategies for successfully directing others to what they want. **This is not an absolute art** , paradoxically *the sale of books to detect manipulators is a chance for those who are really* . Most people who read these books understand that they have been manipulated by a spouse, a family member or what we like to name *toxic people* . In these works, we forget to say that **the manipulator can only play when there is a prey who accepts this dance** . A victim of manipulation, will remain manipulable **if we find his levers** . *The most common mistake is to believe that because we know the tools and techniques, we are protected* . On the contrary, this high opinion of oneself towards the manipulators opens up heaps of exploitable breaches. I love the game of manipulation and it is above all a game. **I am certainly of the worst breed of manipulators, because often, I do not expect an enjoyable return for me, as a reward, but the simple fact of putting the process, in short the spiderweb, and taking the prey in it, is a satisfaction.** It is a respect for the technique and the process that gives me pleasure, often less than the consequences that can be complex to manage sometimes.

What I just presented *gets closer to the workings of the narcissistic perverts* But with the exception that I do not care about the person with whom I use manipulation, I do not want to own or even keep it in a web.

It's only, **the pleasure of seeing the workings put in place** . It scares you or you find me vicious and bastard, if you have this book in your hands, you are not really far from me. Welcome 😊. **I am just as manipulable as the people I handled** and that I will continue to manipulate. **I know we can not avoid manipulation** and the most fun is to realize that we are being manipulated but that we can not do anything, it's too late. It's a bit like in Judo when we have our feet off and it's over, we know we're going to fall. **The world of manipulation makes us humble.** What Humble You do not care about our mouths Pank !!! Since the beginning of the test you are pretentious and kind you make style that you can do everything to others! You dare to speak of humility !!! Yes, *the humility of knowing that we are not the strongest, that we do not always manage to put the wheels in place, that we are manipulated ... Without this humility you will remain those mental consumers of the self defense of the mind, who will always be behind the professionals of manipulation.* We all grew up in the manipulation, often emotional, sometimes physical (for some it was frequently), and mental. I was fortunate to have the panel at home, which gave me a beautiful school and a quality training ground.

We have seen that it is sufficient to work, at first, with the decrease of the judgment factor and that it can be further supported by levers such as kindness, substitution or reciprocity. This last notion is interesting to exploit, it's basically **the debt principle** . *You give to get it.* It goes from a look, a smile, a leaflet, a sample to the agent you are moving forward, the presence for a move, etc. Everything at a price and even if we hear many people say **'You're welcome'** Well, that's wrong.

There is *a subconscious expectation of return, now or later.* When you are in your thoughts and a person hands you a sample with a super nice smile, you have **an interruption of your pattern**, a first lever with the sample and a smile, plus **sympathy** of the intervener. Even if it does not always work, for over 50 years this method is used so the return rate is more positive than the investment. Most of the time, there is a refusal for a simple reason, **the information is not passed as a suggestion,** which means that attention has not been sufficiently captured. For information to become possible suggestions, we need to be able to **exploit the trance**. We must succeed in circumventing the judgment **and become ourselves the judgment of our interlocutor**. As I explained it to you, the trance is the communication between the conscious and the subconscious, if we circumvent the judgment and that we replace it, we offer the desired orientation, leaving only the logical and analytical capacity to intervene.

It is necessary to allow **to the conscious to be present,** it is he who will justify the behavior that has been proposed, because *that he can not accept that this physical action or this thought does not belong to him or in any case that he is not the initiator.* Our goal, as an assumed manipulator, is to change information into suggestion. The suggestion principle is usually oriented towards the positive, the precise and the evolutionary. Nevertheless when you are in a dynamic of influence, you **must keep in mind your goal**. When you decide to steer a trance, it is essential to know where you are heading. The manipulation is **a strategy for obtaining**.

Your information must be directed even before you induce a trance. **All the words and gestures will become important.** It is for this reason that NLP and conversational hypnosis **to be rather 'discreet'** in the sense that it is useful to **Gain someone's trust** of our interlocutors. For this, we have seen that sympathy / kindness is a winning way, it diminishes some defenses, nevertheless you must be in a correctness of use. **Too kind is suspicious** So do not hesitate, when you feel that you are doing too much, to throw a small valve or a spade to make a light **EMOTIONAL ASCENSCEUR** . Many do it spontaneously in the exchanges, there is a compliment where a nice sentence before breaking the model with a little joke. This is a way of keeping the lead on the conversation and especially of **do not leave suspicion** about what you are doing. The opposite method turns out with many people in reaction, opposing everything, winning. By building a communication with *rather aggressive ideas and suggestions, I would say more precisely provocative* . Your partners will stand back and what might seem like a distancing, will be able to *be interrupted by a change of tone, posture and semantics* . In short, the provocateur imbued with him, you will move to a sincerity of attention and history that will hang people. You've probably done that already, when following some virulent and critical exchanges, you feel the atmosphere rotting and you change the subject to return to a sentence of the type: 'I too have already done that' or 'it happens to everyone to make mistakes', to avoid staying in a negative dynamic and you do not manage anymore, *you leave some weight* and you get involved as no different from the person you just criticized.

Emotional lifts are widely used in seduction relationships (Any situation where we sell an image of ourselves to others, and we train each other in this image). We offer **a lead** to our interlocutor vis-à-vis what he is or what he has put in place. In short, you play flattery. Be careful, once again it must be fine and above all do not impose itself as a point that you want to mark. By ratifying the eyes and the body, that is to say by seeking to discover the impact of your words, you will be able to know if your suggestion is passed. The points to observe are the lips, to see the smiles, the eyes to see if there is pleasure, the body if it stands up as to express a pride.

Once **this suggestion has made its way,** you will be able to add a BUT. And suggest ideas that question what you have just boasted about a few minutes ago. This will *change the attention of the conversation and open a breach in the interlocutor.* You will touch the emotions and thus possibly react, open a positive and negative mixture towards you and your arguments. At this point, you need to know where you want to lead the conversation: either you return to positive and feed these suggestions, or you decide to **mark your pitch** and remain neutral so that this less positive message stays in the mind of your interlocutor. *Many people think that manipulating must be done in positive speeches. This is not always the case, sometimes, this doubt that you will put, this disturbing emotion that you will put, will make you a unique person in an interview.* Think about this notion of marketing, it does not matter that we talk about you good or bad, we just have to talk about you, remember you.

You understand well **that playing with the elevator is inductive** because it imposes a return to your emotions that are in the subconscious. Your information then moves to a suggestion, something that will impact now or a little later. **Repetition** will become a particularly important ally in the rest of your exchanges. For the time being, we are going to look a little more at this way of making ourselves ... pleasant vis-à-vis the people we wish to manipulate ... Do you feel the dark side evolve in you?

4 / Create trust in others

We are not all equal when it comes to human interactions. Whether we want it or not, genetics help us or not. *The physical is the first thing that manipulates the idea that we are going to make people.* After we realized that the dress code could go around this criterion a bit, but **ATTITUDE** is not adjusted, it will pass quickly and the illusion will disappear. Did you know that a person who is considered beautiful will find a job easier than someone who is not. No need to look far, we will always pay more attention to a child who is beautiful and cute than another. We will let more things go to the 'cute' ones. This is unfortunately so well understood by men and women with the advantageous physique that they often use this lever for many years. How many exquisite women begin to panic towards midlife when a new generation puts them in the closet and the only thing that allowed them to live well was not their head but their bodies. It is a sad reality that affects men less, who sometimes with time develop **a charm** ... rarely do we hear about the charm of fifty-year-old women unlike men. We are in a world of compensation and even more manipulative strategy.

To achieve what we want in our daily lives, with the qualities we have. The most dangerous manipulators are those who are already beautiful genetically and who have moreover **developed the intelligence of manipulation** . Nevertheless even if we are not in this 'elite' this does not prevent anything. The mastery of **the science of manipulation** you will get enough satisfaction not to, or for less, worry about what you missed at the base.

I have the belief that **we are purely perfect** as we are. We have defects compensated by qualities, and it's up to us to make the most of our potentials, rather than focusing on what can not be changed. The first thing we can really work on, when we want to influence, is **attitude** that we are going to have. It is always useful to develop **a social intelligence** . There is no need to love humans for that, just *understand the codes of the different groups* that we cross. The simplest is to find the one that will be considered as the alpha, that is to say the dominant group. It will give you the 'type' of acting and you will understand how others work with this type of energy. In general, if there are people around and people, even if they do not specifically like it, stay around, that's *that there are enough levers used to 'hypnotize' the group* . It is for this reason, that many build a form of social conformism, the more I look like the group or the interlocutor in these codes, the more I can be integrated into his model of life.

This avoids a possible confrontation with a 'world' that he does not want to discover. The first thing to do once you have a clear goal in mind is to go to the contact. It's with **your physical attitude and your look** that you will propose acceptable terms, where not, to those present. A prince does not have the attitudes of a hiphop singer and a DG of a big box not those of a startup in new technologies. It is up to us to adapt our attitude to the figure of authority, if it is in a group or with our interlocutor face to face. **The look** *is the first step of taking lead.* Take the lead is the concept of leading the game, you *take a step ahead* the interlocutor, without necessarily being aware of it.

It's like in some sports, if we gain a few centimeters or a half-second, we take a lead that **can be decisive** in the following events. In this manipulative art, you look for the person you want to manipulate. Parents often do so with the history of big eyes. They completely change their attitude and start to make big eyes, seek contact with the child. It is also the case with first moments of seduction, when a man or a woman keeps the contact a few moments. The initiator of the action, if the other does not turn his head or lower his eyes out of interest, has taken a point for the approach and the link that can be put in place. An error that is often conveyed is that of taking the lead on the handshake, during a meeting or an interview.

In reality if the other has already connected you with the look, you have taken a long time. Once the first contact is proposed, it is useful to enter the world of your interlocutors. **A manipulator must be interested** , and if it really does not bother you, act as if. This step is **taking information** on the one hand, concerning the subjects who build positive emotions and those who seem less to pack it. We keep it in mind for the eventual **emotional lift** . This is also what NLP serves us as a connection. **We are slowly entering the physical and mental territory** of the interlocutor, taking the precaution of not going too much in intimacy, as much at the level of the proxemia, that is to say the distance between you two, than in the stories told. Interest is not really investigating, otherwise you risk, especially in the first meetings *to be a little intrusive* . You know this feeling when a loved one wants to be interested in what we have done and we are not inclined to share information, this feeling that he tries to enter a world that does not concern them, *for the moment* .

Just remember that when the time or situation becomes more open, there is a good chance, with an indirect question, of taking the information you want. This will happen when your partner is in his **false lead phase** , that is to say when he speaks for a long time. As I pointed out, we are not equal before nature.

Only, *we can adapt so much to nature* others, that we can make ourselves forget what we look like, to give an image of ourselves that others want to see. Once again, this will be possible through **induction** that we will set up, once the contact and the report installed. You will be able to make **mirroring,** that is to say resume verbal and physical behavior, so that he can have the feeling of being heard, understood and especially accepted in these codes. *Do not sing especially* , just imagine that you are dancing, if he speaks softly, look for the sweetness in you, if he moves a lot, move as well. *Give it the impression of being in a known world* , which will reduce apprehension. The inductive element is triggered with the questions. If you are questioning you have a time to get in touch, take some information for a next question and start your mirroring. In addition, little by little, you put your partner in a situation of **'false lead'** . He can easily think that he is leading the situation. You will notice that the alphas sometimes a little too much of them, cut the floor, wish to be at the center of the conversation and sell their ideas and stories. These are the ones *that you can most easily orient* if you do not get into a cock fight. A key point to remember is that **the posture of questioner is the most advantageous in a world of manipulation and influence.**

With the question you have the most powerful weapon of guidance strategies and suggestions. When you ask questions **you are in Pace** .

In NLP, we explain that *it is the one who follows. The confusion that many people make is to believe that it is the lead that puts us in a strong position,* because the other one can not place one and we can get lots of suggestions. Even if sometimes it's true, because we **sature and we repeat** many times the ideas for integrating them is not necessarily the most subtle strategy. How many of you, to make others feel guilty, ask questions so that the other person gets tangled up and lets go of the mistakes that have been made. A deceived woman will rarely tell her husband, you have deceived me on such and such day, but where were you? Whom etc. **The question pushes to the fault** and manipulative as you are, how many times have you pushed others into their entrenchments with questions and a little complementary phrase like, 'I just ask a question ...'. By asking the questions, you now know that you are proposing **an internal focus** so you can join **a suggestion** . So you have every interest *when you created the report, ask questions* which will give the other something to express themselves. Avoid closed questions, that is, answered by yes or no. Open the questions so that the other can take the time *to expose his ideas* . From time to time take the lead, to show that you have a presence and it also allows you to take the ideas and semantics of your interlocutor to show that you understand, that you have the same language. You have certainly validated the ideas and words of people you wanted to seduce.

This is so common that in couples, some people take years to say that in fact, he does not like this or that thing. This acceptance of the world of the other often leads to *to lies or, as some like to say, arrangements with reality* . All shots are allowed to achieve what we want. I imagine, the passive manipulators blow and say that they clearly are not like that, what matters is the pleasure of others. Let others go before this kind of nauseating ploys. They are often the specialists, so that others have confidence in them. One of their value is *keep their commitments and the word given is important.* They give confidence by using a strategy similar to the one I just outlined. For them, kindness and reciprocity are levers of everyday life, and allow a powerful relationship. At the slightest need shared by you or supposed of theirs , *they build a report* . They come into contact with a smile, a gesture, an attention or other. They will quickly ask if it's okay, if they can help you, if you want more or more, that is to say that they directly put themselves in place. You, you will focus on you, on what you want. Which causes *an interruption of pattern.* From there, they try to become an indispensable element under the idea of kindness and presence, they try to place themselves as referents. You remember the figure of authority, it's his cousin, it's being 'the only' person doing this for you etc ... Nevertheless even if it is sold as a free service, there are clauses. This point in the contract, *it's reciprocity* , make me different with attention, thank you, a "you're the best", "we do not make two like you". We become nourishers of their discomfort with indifference. A manipulation that is common and much more pernicious than it seems. My manipulative friends, this is an important step: to create trust and exploit gaps.

5 / Create gaps

Nobody is protected against manipulators and *Protection experts are often former victims who are growing wings*. I remember one intervention once, from someone who told me that I was an expert on the narcissistic perverts because her ex was one of those guys and she got out of it. We become experts in the management of rape when we have been raped? This is a manipulation that opens **breaches** on people who live these manipulations in everyday life and who will give their trust to this type of people. They play with **the authority figure and a congruence / coherence report** . It is easy to pass as a figure of authority when we resume his story and we are out of the problem. Very often we only know **romanced story** of this figure. Take into account that there can be no authority figure *only from the moment we give someone the opportunity to be on a pedestal* . **We are also responsible for letting ourselves slip into the game of manipulators.** Perhaps by repetition of a model of life, my father was violent so I choose only violent men, perhaps for fun of the game of departure as it seems to control. Whatever motivations, which are multiple, we accept the deal of manipulation. **If you are manipulated, chances are you accepted it** , call it naivete or bullshit, you have fueled the relationship, by not leaving the game. I know, I'm obnoxious, nevertheless I like the idea of Karpman who proposes his dramatic triangle *there is no executioner unless there is a victim* and not far can drag a savior, besides the executioner often, in the manipulative act, this first cap.

If you keep that in mind, *you will be wary of saviors* ... or examples that I gave in the previous chapter. A savior can quickly become a hangman. **The savior of manipulators** poses as a figure of authority and then he puts forward his life story, **consistent with** with the tools he offers you. As you see there *potential realization,* you will find this famous mirroring and you will engage in the approach that is proposed, *difficult after coming back on* and to say that it is naze or worse that we were manipulated by the person who promised us to get out of it. *The **breach** often plays on the **doubt** and the **projection**.* This is what is powerful in the approach of people who tell you, do like me and you will see it works. They make you believe that you are exactly like them and that 'if it works on me ... so why not you?' How many times have you tried diets or activities while waiting for amazing results because one of your friends sold you a dream? This is also one of the great levers of meetings that were called in the past tupperware, the network of friends to whom projections are sold. As *manipulator more and more end* you will conduct your investigation on the breaches of your interlocutors. As I told you, avoid doing it in the beginning, you will see that many people, once in confidence, talk a lot. In reality it is a form of **yes set.** Initially the 'yes set' is *stimulation of the brain so that you are more inclined towards an affirmative notion*. We propose closed questions that will lead you to think yes. You read this book, you wonder about the coherence of this book, you continue to read these lines ... maybe you start to like the science of manipulation. Leading to 'yes' *, it may be that my last suggestion leads to a 'yes'*.

We use it very regularly in everyday life to convince by avoiding that the other can not place one, and to pose as an obvious **the key suggestion** you want to impose. When you put yourself in and ask questions, when *you have spotted the topics that extol* your partner, so let him talk for a while, he's opening up to a pattern, a fluid communication model and so he's open to questions. The most interesting thing is that once *that he will be confident and happy in his sharing* , you can ask him about the subjects *which he was not open* to communicate at the beginning of the communication. He has taken a 'habit' of talking, generating information and interrupting it, will put him in a vacuum, especially if **you stay in a pace, a posture of questioner** .

The mistake is to fill the void. Do not do it, it is precisely the other who will be the most uncomfortable in this void that he filled so few moments earlier with conviction, he will give at least some information that opens **a breach** to have more, just because he wants to talk about it at that time.

This' yes set 'becomes an orientation that I call' creating a **CURRENT'** , you have set up a flow that will be difficult for your interlocutor to stop. Why? Simply because the human has a favorite subject, himself. Some people will tell you that they do not like to talk about them, *you have not asked the right questions and you have not touched on the right topics* . A breach in a dam will cause the water to pass, even if it means giving up your dam. Afterwards we will use a kind of jackhammer, a tool that we all know when we teach or educate. **Repetition** .

When there is a doubt or a breach, your manipulative role is to **nurture these ideas** as much as possible, so that your ideas fit into the spirit of the one who converses with you. In hypnosis, we like to talk about **seeding** to plant the seed in the subconscious of the other. It's because of *the use of the trance and therefore the decrease of judgment* that you will be able to put this seed through a suggestion. This will produce **a breach** on which you will return. To put it simply, you will plant an idea and you will **come back many times over** in different ways, whether through laughter, emotional lift, referrals, kindness, exchange.

You have a multitude of ways to do it. Humor is often used to lighten the idea while nourishing it. Have you ever repeated one of your desires to your loved ones in the hope that they will respond? With this little slack who says "who tries nothing has nothing". It is certain that if you only have one conversation to influence, you will have to support the idea. For that you have two powerful tools in your arsenal.

Tonal variation and spatial anchoring . The tonal variation, you put it in place in all your conversations, you press on certain words, certain emotions or remarks that *you want to make different from the flow of your word.* To put it simply, you can pass a suggestion with your interlocutor in a trance. **lowering your tone at the end of the sentence** . Looking to **focus** what you're saying, because your partner's attention will be **follow** the voice and so *to pay more attention* . So that will allow *to the idea of taking place,* even if at first, it will certainly not be validated.

You can sometimes insert a pattern break and an immediate suggestion, by raising your tone of voice and thus change the pace of the discussion to get your idea across. The simplest *it is to tell a story in substitution.* You invent the situation that interests you through an imaginary friend to whom it happened and from then on *your substitution will allow you to give focus and tonal variations as you wish.* **An anchor** is *an association that we make or put in place to a person, between an emotional state and a point of recall,* often a gesture or a word. In the case of spatial anchoring, it is to observe well the person with whom you talk to define in which direction he directs his eyes when he is in a positive emotion and to make a gesture that corresponds, type a finger who gets up. Do the same to know where he looks when he is in less positive states and hold him back. You can possibly tie it to another gesture, such as a finger that gets up with the other hand, the side he's been watching. This will allow you to play on unconscious emotional lifts where appropriate. This technique will ask you to **attention and observation**, an assumed manipulator sets up a conscious science that demands a **true concentration**. If you find yourself standing up and have noticed that, for example, the person you are chatting with, looking down on the left when he speaks to you about a negative element, be careful to shift yourself from this location during the discussion for *avoid that it refocuses on*. On the other hand if it speaks to you of pleasant things and that it raises its eyes by looking on the right, do not hesitate to take place towards this zone, that will impose on his glance to remain in a assimilated strategy *to a well-being and therefore associate it with you*.

When you have managed to create gaps, it remains to keep your goal in mind and to offer suggestions that will feed the idea that you have implanted.

Always take a moment to ratify, that is to say to check the partner's reactions, if you feel that you are getting too heavy, put aside your strategy and allow him to return to a positive lead by making him talk about what he likes most.

6 / The power of the projection

Offer your interlocutors the dream and, in general, it's not your place to make them dream but let them go in what they build as their own film. When you are in your manipulation, do not hesitate to become **transition object** for your interlocutors. **A projective surface** what they think, even if what they think, of you, of your ideas or others, is wrong. You let them go *in touch with their imaginations* and in a trance that you will be able to reorient. It is for this reason that *we need to build reports fast enough, to take information* . We could say that it is useful to point it to positive and as I suggested to you later, it is not a necessity. A negative projection on you, a person who does not like you or finds you con, remains only a perception suggested by feedback on types like you, at the physical, clothing or semantic level. It is a 'subjective experience' that leads to this idea. Have you ever had a negative feeling about a person and after a discussion, you see it completely differently. Well, **you were manipulated, the projection** and phrases like 'there are only idiots who do not change their minds', 'you have to be ready to welcome new experiences' or just 'you have to be open' are blessed bread for the manipulators.

There are many returns that show, that with sometimes decades, this person whom we had not felt at the first glance, makes us a dirty blow ... We are much smarter than we sometimes want to recognize. One of the strategies is to play with **the lack** information. In general, **the lever of lack** the result of saying that there is a limited stock for consumers to rush.

On a more advanced idea, just take the information on *the elements that give this negative projection on you, to express the idea that it lacks information about who you really are and not about the image you give* . The mistake that is classic is to tell the other that something is missing, as if we were a limited stock. This clumsy interaction makes the person even prettier. On the other hand, listen to the objections and the presupposed ideas, they can **to be questioned** (our favorite posture), and to bring the idea that it misses elements and not to give them when the person is interested, will leave his projection to imagine new possible models. More generally, when you ask your suggestions think not to be too precise. We have already seen this idea of nonspecific vis-à-vis a possible future or a negotiation, a product or just an output can be multiplied if you let the other imagine what it will be able to give. Once you have captured the **motivation and envy,** it is enough to take again the ideas which are exposed to you, as in phase of mirroring, and to amplify them. To this you exalt the whole with a playful tonal variation, some anchors, as well as *elevators by mounting the bearings* .

When you propose an idea or suggestion, you do not sell an object, you sell an experience, an inner stimulation. Whether you, a concept or a product that you want to put forward, it is the projection and the imagined perception that will have importance. *We know that the real changes according to the emotional state,* an innocuous gift becomes full of values when it has been associated (anchored) with a powerful internal experience. Are you able to create emotions in the people you come in contact with?

7 / Juggling with emotions

I offered you the principle of **the emotional lift** it's a technique of **classic hot-cold** to play with emotions. It's important to keep in mind that some people are *in the mental center and that they may seem airtight to emotions*. Most of the time the lever to use is **the fear**, nevertheless it is possible to play with their ease at **to project oneself into the future**. You understood in the previous chapter that this offers a possibility on perceptions. *If you nurture this principle in the minds, you will be able to meet their emotions and feed them to orient them to new ideas.* All you need is **lay anchors** and pay attention to note the positive emotions in order to exploit them. The dialogue risks remaining on a very logical and analytical language, you will have to play on the emotions and you will have few returns on the ratification, it will have to be even more observant. For most of the other people you are going to look for, you can take into account **basic emotions: fear, anger, joy, sadness, surprise, scorn, disgust.** As part of the manipulation, according to your objectives, you will categorize into two groups, the **positive and negative emotions**. You keep in mind that for the elevator you **alternate** or pass each time a floor for **bring to a climax**. Fear, anger, sadness, even disgust are easy emotions to make live. A person caught in a negative emotion is in a trance. It's harder for them to keep **an objective capacity of judgment.** This is often useful when you want to guide a decision. You open a **idea of insecurity** on one of the choices or an emotion of rejection of an idea to validate the one you propose.

In the options that you will propose, think of anchoring them with negative emotions. The last option with positive marking if possible should be your choice. The brain is lazy enough and most of the time retains the last element. Easier still if the first proposed elements cause a negative emotion **. anchoring** that we put previously also allows us to make diverse associations with the emotions that interest us. Can you **associate with positive emotions** by a gesture, a touch or a word. That's why sometimes we feel good with some people without knowing why, often they were there during a period when we were particularly good, without having any particular links. We associated it with positive emotions. The manipulator will make sure to be associated, then initiator of positive emotions. You will create surprise emotions and joy, to open the trance and give suggestions. Emotions are common, they can easily make you lose some of the strategies we've put in place. If you want to act with the emotions, it is essential to work on them at first. Master them so that they do not take you away when an interlocutor lives them.

Empathy is one of the most striking techniques of emotional manipulation . We are connected to each other, so we find rapport, mirroring, pace and lead Unlike sympathy, normally (I insist on this term) we do not live the emotions of the other, we have a trance common without the emotional suggestions of the other imply us. We are in his world, in the right understanding, **without 'side' effects** of his emotions. We can take over the lead and, thanks to this hyperlink, direct to new ideas and suggestions.

The interlocutor really has the feeling that we understand it perfectly and it is not totally false, except that we do not suffer or are not stimulated in the same way, we are apt to have **a judgment factor** Where there is no longer. Remember the number of times you were empathetic and you took power over the other to point to what you thought was more gentle or soothing. Bravo ! it gives a beautiful image of therapists, is not it? 😊

Conclusion

My friends **assumed manipulators,** I'm going to dwell on these few elements so that you can **put them into practice.** To think that you are a good manipulator without putting your art on the ground every day is just to manipulate yourself by reading only books. If you do that, you will be like self-defenders of the mind, who will understand that they have been manipulated but too late. *It is not because you have recognized techniques you know, spontaneously or studied, that you control them.* . **It is impossible not to communicate and as all communication is influence, it is impossible not to manipulate.** The difference, between **passive manipulators and assumed** is the quality of the manipulation. We are all capable of running, yet we are not all able to pass under the 10 seconds to the hundred meters. There are powerful influencers and there are those who galley. In this essay, I gave you simple and usable techniques on all terrains, whether personal, emotional or professional. You have the ability to be a real jerk at every interaction. You will simply notice that if manipulation is natural its voluntary mastery requires discipline and strategy. This is an effort at every encounter, in all the interactions you put in place. You will certainly realize that the results are not always up to the effort.

You will sometimes find that orienting, so that there is a benefit for both parties, can bring much more than for oneself. **But above all do not do it** Be selfish, be assholes, manipulate without thinking of good or evil.

In another essay, I will talk about the strategies and the effectiveness of negation, the attention to be paid to sex and the trances of desire and even waiting. One last thing, to assume by projecting is good, to become aware **of responsibility** what we have in our interactions with others, the impact of our words, our questions, our verbal and nonverbal communications is even more important. **If assuming to be an asshole, you realized that being a good person in his manipulations, it requires consciousness so maybe I would be a happy asshole.**

Le Chesnay, 24th April 2019.

Pank

Who is Christophe Pank ?

I am French and live in Paris. I have worked in hypnosis, NPL, personal development and energetic healing for more than a decade. Everyday, I share my experience and knowledge. To optimise my work, I created HnO (Hype-N-Ose) Hypnose in 2010. As psycho-practitioner, I can help people to learn about themselves, to increase their knowledge. I am now sharing my ideas in essays, videos and audios. The more you open your mind to different ways of thinking, the more you develop your capacity to become who you really are.

Take the time to watch my english Youtube Channel : hnohypnosis and my website : www.hnohypnosis.com